ENTERPRISE

I0139761

Brian Parks

BROADWAY PLAY PUBLISHING INC
New York
www.broadwayplaypublishing.com
info@broadwayplaypublishing.com

First edition: September 2018
I S B N: 978-0-88145-797-1

Book design: Marie Donovan
Page make-up: Adobe InDesign
Typeface: Palatino

ENTERPRISE premiered on 2 February 2017, at the Brick Theater, Brooklyn, New York, produced by Gemini CollisionWorks with the following cast and creative contributors:

LANDRY .... Adam Files
OWENS..Alyssa Simon
SANDERS .... Fred Backus
WEAVER.. Derrick Peterson

Director.. Ian W Hill
Scenic design............................ Ian W Hill & Berit Johnson
Costumes.. Kaitlyn Day
Lighting design .... Ian W Hill
Music design.. Ian W Hill
Props design...Berit Johnson
Production stage manager .... Berit Johnson

ENTERPRISE was subsequently produced—in its
current, revised version—at Assembly's George
Square Studio 2 at the 2017 Edinburgh Festival Fringe,
produced by Americana Absurdum Productions with
the following cast and creative contributors:

LANDRY .... Brian Dykstra
OWENS .... Jonathan Fishman
SANDERS .... Christopher Carley
WEAVER .... Matthew Boston

Director .... David Calvitto
Sound design .... David Calvitto & Kari Berntson
Lighting design .... Max Grano De Oro
Costume design .... Robin Gurin
Set design .... Margarett Perry
Prop design .... Berit Johnson
Production stage manager .... Margarett Perry
Board operator .... Adam Toussaint

CHARACTERS & SETTING

LANDRY, *a businessperson*
OWENS, *a businessperson*
SANDERS, *a businessperson*
WEAVER, *a businessperson*

The four businesspeople all wear business clothes that are close in appearance but not identical. Gender, age, race of actors/characters is flexible. In production, adjust gender of pronouns, etc., as necessary.

A black stage. Set pieces very minimal: four black chairs, maybe a couple black desks, all easily movable and used as the director sees fit. A sense that the stage is isolated in space. The playing areas for each scene should be tightly delineated by the lighting. The scenes should be acted in a quick, propulsive manner, with the exception of some of the late-night scenes. Quick sound cues between scenes where the director desires.

Scene titles are for rehearsal and reference purposes only, and should not be used in production.

Scene
"Arriving"

(Lights rise on the stage. LANDRY, OWENS, SANDERS, and WEAVER are all inside an elevator, a couple of them carrying business folders. They press the button, and the elevator begins rising to a very high floor in a very tall building.)

WEAVER: The market will be good today.

SANDERS: No way.

WEAVER: I can feel it in my ears.

OWENS: Me too.

LANDRY: That's the air-pressure change in this elevator.

OWENS: Market's going way up, just like we are now.

SANDERS: *(Disagreeing)* Too much uncertainty.

LANDRY: Experts are betting against the dollar.

WEAVER: Against the dollar?

OWENS: That's insane.

WEAVER: The dollar's going up, just like this elevator.

LANDRY: This elevator is rising, resisting the force of gravity.

WEAVER: If gravity ceased, elevator companies would be right out of business.

SANDERS: He's right.

OWENS: All kinds of companies.

(Brief pause)

LANDRY: *(To* WEAVER*)* What's the forecast on gravity?

(Quick blackout)

Scene
"Conferences"

(LANDRY, OWENS, SANDERS, *and* WEAVER *in their office conference room.* WEAVER *is gesturing forward, out the "window".)*

WEAVER: Conferences in town.

LANDRY: Yeah?

SANDERS: Big ones.

OWENS: People in hotels.

WEAVER: Walking the streets.

SANDERS: Carrying maps.

OWENS: Pointing at things.

WEAVER: Looking up at buildings.

LANDRY: Mispronouncing street names.

OWENS: People going to presentations.

WEAVER: Sitting in chairs.

LANDRY: On diases.

SANDERS: Speakers—

WEAVER: Examining developments.

SANDERS: Fiscal years.

OWENS: Using handouts.

LANDRY: People like handouts.

WEAVER: Need 'em.

OWENS: A conference without handouts—

SANDERS: No one comes back next year.

WEAVER: Distribute product samples.

LANDRY: Like souvenirs.

OWENS: "Souvenir" is French for "remember."

LANDRY: It's why the French never forget anything.

WEAVER: Name tags.

OWENS: Coffee urns.

SANDERS: Pastries.

OWENS: Slide shows—

WEAVER: Making analyses.

LANDRY: With graphs.

SANDERS: Parabolas.

OWENS: F'n parabolas.

(Quick blackout)

Scene
"Print-outs"

(LANDRY, OWENS, SANDERS, *and* WEAVER *are looking at some print-outs.)*

LANDRY: Who made these copies?

OWENS: I did.

WEAVER: They're off-center.

SANDERS: They're just for us.

LANDRY: Do we look off-center?

OWENS: No.

LANDRY: Something wrong with our longitude today?

OWENS: *(Defensively)* Okay—

WEAVER: Then why are you giving us off-center copies?

OWENS: They're just for now.

(Pause)

LANDRY: *(Thrusting copies at* OWENS*)* Take them back.

OWENS: What?

LANDRY: Take them back whence they came.

SANDERS: *(To* OWENS, *with angry emphasis)* Whence they came!

(Quick blackout)

Scene
"Philosophy"

*(*SANDERS *and* WEAVER*)*

SANDERS: And that's your philosophy?

WEAVER: Every tenet.

SANDERS: You live by it always?

WEAVER: I live by it *usually.*

SANDERS: Not always?

WEAVER: I sometimes lapse to get perspective on its genius.

SANDERS: Where did this philosophy come from?

WEAVER: Germany, most of it. Germany is full of solid thinkers, men with a firm grip on the ineffable.

SANDERS: I need a philosophy.

WEAVER: Choose wisely. The wrong philosophy will cook you into a stew of doubt and debauchery.

SANDERS: Debauchery?

WEAVER: A life of evil. Of terrible evil you look forward to every day.

(Quick blackout)

Scene
"Oil Painting"

(LANDRY *and* OWENS. OWENS *holds up a framed oil painting, showing it to* LANDRY. *The painting's back is to the audience. The audience never sees the actual image.)*

LANDRY: What's that, Owens?

OWENS: An oil painting of the Chairman.

LANDRY: I hear from upstairs he's in a weird mood today.

OWENS: He won't be after he sees how I painted him.

LANDRY: You did this?

OWENS: Yep.

LANDRY: *(Pointing at painting)* It's so life-like.

OWENS: Thanks.

LANDRY: The sideburns—

OWENS: A special gray pigment.

LANDRY: The lapels—

OWENS: Can almost feel the wool.

LANDRY: The dead pheasants—

OWENS: He hunts, I'm sure of it!

LANDRY: He plays the lute?

OWENS: Like all the powerful. If the Chairman likes it, every business person will want one for their boss. People will collect my work. Wild bidding at auction houses, people raising paddles or tanned fingers. My paintings hanging over fireplaces in country mansions that smell of port and springer spaniel.

LANDRY: I like those distant mountains.

OWENS: That's symbolism.

LANDRY: "Symbolism"?

OWENS: Stuff that means what it isn't.

LANDRY: Sounds confusing.

OWENS: Symbolism is confusion for the greater good.
You care about mankind's soul?

LANDRY: Sure.

OWENS: Take a second look at symbolism.

(Quick blackout)

Scene
"Paper Clip"

*(WEAVER and OWENS. Both are holding documents.
OWENS is sniffing the air, a little puzzled.)*

WEAVER: *(Confused re OWENS's sniffing)* What is it?

OWENS: *(Sniffs again, then unconcerned)* Nothing. *(Then
re his documents)* You got a paper clip?

WEAVER: *(Proudly producing one)* The paper clip. In
Dutch—"little trombone."

OWENS: Because of the shape.

WEAVER: They look like trombones.

OWENS: To Dutch people.

WEAVER: Some things never became office supplies.

OWENS: Yeah?

WEAVER: Like oboes.

OWENS: Sure.

WEAVER: Reed instruments in general.

OWENS: Rocks.

WEAVER: Right! To ancient man, a rock had great
utility. But in the modern office nobody ever requests

one. *(Pause, then imitating office workers.)* "Hey, I left a rock in your inbox." *(Pause)* "A need your rock by three P M. Hear me?" *(Pause)* "Hear me?!"

(Quick blackout)

Scene
"The Watch"

(LANDRY and SANDERS)

LANDRY: And taxes, Sanders. We can't get nailed on taxes. The government sticking its long arm into our cash and using it to fund—what? Their bonuses. Handouts to low-achievers. Sometimes the government builds a road. Okay, that's all right. But some of those roads go to black sites.

SANDERS: Black sites?

LANDRY: *Black sites.* Places where even the President doesn't know what goes on. You think something *good* happens there? You think they use black sites to make ice cream? Bunch of guys with code names at the end of an unmarked road turning handles all day to make a refreshing treat?

(Suddenly SANDERS's watch chime goes off. It plays "Old MacDonald.")

LANDRY: What's that sound?

SANDERS: Oh, sorry. Just my watch.

LANDRY: Your watch?

SANDERS: Yeah—the chime thing.

LANDRY: *(Disparaging)* That's a nursery rhyme.

SANDERS: What?

LANDRY: That's a nursery rhyme song.

SANDERS: No it isn't.

LANDRY: It's *Old MacDonald.*

SANDERS: *(Turning it off)* What?

LANDRY: *Old MacDonald.*

SANDERS: It's just a chime sound.

LANDRY: *(Not singing)* Old MacDonald had a farm, E-I-E-I-O.

SANDERS: Huh?

LANDRY: *(Now singing to demonstrate)* Old MacDonald had a farm, E-I-E-I-O. And on this farm he had a cow, E-I-E-I-O. With a moo-moo here—

SANDERS: *(Not singing, honestly puzzled, not knowing song or tune)* A moo-moo there?

LANDRY: Here a moo—

SANDERS: *(Not singing, still puzzled)* There a moo?

LANDRY: Everywhere a moo-moo.

(Brief pause)

SANDERS: *(Somewhat disturbed by* LANDRY*)* Yeah, I don't think so.

(Quick blackout)

Scene
"Skyscrapers"

*(*OWENS *and* WEAVER *stand forward downstage, looking out a window.)*

OWENS: Quite the view, Weaver.

WEAVER: Tremendous.

OWENS: From these windows so high up here.

WEAVER: *(Pointing)* Even those strange gathering clouds—

OWENS: Look amazing.

WEAVER: The vistas—

OWENS: A miracle.

WEAVER: No, Owens, not a miracle.

OWENS: But look at it—

WEAVER: Not a miracle, Sanders, because *we* did this. *Business* built this view. That's what business *does*. Builds towers that reach into the atmosphere, towers with glass entrances and soaring lobbies of polished marble, the fruit of our greatest quarries! Elevator banks—elevator after elevator, buttons ready to be pressed, each glowing with mystery. Who knows what button 15 leads to, button 20, 50, or 85! Who was the man whose brain first fired a Neolithic synapse and thought of adding a *second floor* to his crude hut? Who took his eyes off the horizon and looked *up*. A second floor, then a third, a fourth—till we get architects kissing the heavens with pointy needles, then epic rectangles of glass. These architects were geniuses, men with more talent in their silver mustaches than the rest of us put together. Visions came to them, edifices so tall they can be seen for miles, by grocers and mailmen, farmers looking up from their plows and wishing they could work in them, away from their manure and poorly dressed wives. And atop these skyscrapers they attach radio towers. Radio waves throbbing to every horizon. But traveling upward, too—into space! Through the ring of planets and great cold ether, the dark void, speeding through the heavens and white-and-orange galaxies, searching for anyone to receive their signal. *Anyone!* Till finally—finally! —they hit a planet unimagined by our best astronomers. A planet inhabited by creatures whose bodies contain not a single element from our periodic table, whose house pets resemble great balls of cottage cheese. But a race besotted with the power of radio! Their landscapes cluttered with antennae, their homes ablaze with dials and knobs, gathered together every night with their offspring, glued to broadcasts from across their globe. And that's how they're sitting the night their broadcast starts to crackle and hiss, then turn to a kind of static, then into *something they've never heard before.* They hear *us!* The consonants and vowels of their language cannot describe it. But they know—they *know* they have heard a sound from *across space,* from a vastly distant planet. They know now they are *not alone!* They hush those balls of cottage cheese and listen to the signals and begin to quiver and shake, then melt a little as they do when excited. They stand and jump in celebration, hugging and melting on each other. Then they go quiet and separate. They stand still and lift their odd optic nerves toward the sky, to their heavens. They reach out and clasp their...claspers, giving thanks for the sound coming from their radio. A sound that started atop a skyscraper—a country song about a pickup truck loaded with beer and hope.

(Quick blackout)

Scene
"Budget Cut"

(LANDRY, OWENS, SANDERS, *and* WEAVER. LANDRY *has just entered, very agitated.)*

LANDRY: The budget has been cut!

WEAVER: What?

LANDRY: The budget has been cut.

OWENS: By who?

LANDRY: Someone upstairs!

OWENS: Goddamnit!

LANDRY: Someone upstairs with their head so far up their ass they're licking their own small intestine.

OWENS: This is a bad sign.

WEAVER: *Bad.*

OWENS: A warning.

LANDRY: An omen.

SANDERS: An augury.

WEAVER: A what?

SANDERS: An augury, dammit!

OWENS: *(angered)* What could they be thinking?!

LANDRY: At this time in the quarter!

WEAVER: The board are idiots.

LANDRY: Cretins.

OWENS: They're such morons even morons think they're morons!

LANDRY: We have to go and tell the Chairman.

SANDERS: What?!

LANDRY: Go up to his floor and warn him.

OWENS: The Chairman?!

LANDRY: That the budget committee is out of control.

WEAVER: Right now!

OWENS: *(Arguing against)* But it's the Chairman!

SANDERS: *(Re LANDRY)* He's right—

LANDRY: Tell him *what's really going on!*

WEAVER: We have to go up to that floor and down the hall—

LANDRY: And tell him the truth!

SANDERS: He'll stop this idiocy.

OWENS: *(Now convinced too)* This folly.

LANDRY: This nincompoovia!

SANDERS: To the Chairman!

WEAVER: The Chairman!

ALL: The Chairman!

(Quick blackout)

Scene
"Pissed Pants"

(After a moment or two, LANDRY, OWENS, SANDERS, *and* WEAVER *all enter. As they enter, it's clear that all four have pissed their pants—big wet stains in each person's crotch area. They stand around all looking sheepish and uncomfortable, occasionally glancing down at themselves or at one of the other's wet stain. This goes on for a bit, then* OWENS *speaks.)*

OWENS: That was scary.

WEAVER: I've never seen—

SANDERS: No.

LANDRY: I've never seen the Chairman so angry.

(Pause)

OWENS: The way he looked at us.

WEAVER: It was…

OWENS: *(At loss for words)* I couldn't…I…

(Pause. They all look at one another's stains again.)

WEAVER: That was a bad walk just now. A bad walk through the office.

OWENS: They were all looking.

(Brief pause)

SANDERS: It's going to be in the office newsletter.

OWENS: We shouldn't have all walked back together.

(Pause)

OWENS: I'd like to go home.

WEAVER: No time.

SANDERS: Me to.

WEAVER: It's just us in here. Doesn't matter now.

SANDERS: I'm getting prickly.

LANDRY: We need to get back to work. All of us.

OWENS: I don't like the odor.

SANDERS: Me either.

OWENS: Bad.

LANDRY: No. No, this is what *successful* companies smell like. Companies with good, tough leaders. People at great companies are *always* walking around like this. It was no fun up there, but this place needs it. *(Pointing to his trousers)* This should happen every day. We should hope this happens again tomorrow, and the day after that, and the day after that—because *that's* when this company has won! *(Indicating everyone's stains)* This is why we went to business school!!

(Quick blackout)

Scene
"Multiples"

(LANDRY, OWENS, SANDERS, *and* WEAVER)

OWENS: Our multiples!

LANDRY: What?

OWENS: Our multiples are shrinking—

SANDERS: Jesus.

WEAVER: How do you know?

LANDRY: There's nothing on the ticker—

WEAVER: Or word from upstairs.

SANDERS: Owens can smell them.

OWENS: I can smell our multiples when they change—

WEAVER: *(Incredulous)* No.

OWENS: It's in the air!

LANDRY: Not possible.

OWENS: *(Indicating a direction)* I thought I was smelling something before. Coming from that way—the scent of disappearing value!

WEAVER: But—

OWENS: A low acrid odor—

LANDRY: I smell nothing—

SANDERS: *(To* LANDRY *re* OWENS*)* Only *he* can!

OWENS: Atoms of loss drifting in the wind! Floating up my nostrils and hitting my nose hairs, clinging hard to the follicles. Then more, wafting from a stock meltdown in markets there— *(Points off one direction.)* And there too! *(Points off a different direction.)* The atoms breaking off and hitting my mucus membrane, which panics and tells the cilia, putting the cilia in an uproar, who cry out to the axons, who send pulses to the olfactory bulb—

LANDRY, WEAVER, & SANDERS: *(Together) Bulb!*

LANDRY: Something *is* going on!

SANDERS: Christ.

WEAVER: *(Warily)* Something really, really big.

(All four stand there, each looking a different direction anxiously. Then quick blackout.)

Scene
"Panicking Board"

(LANDRY, OWENS, *and* SANDERS. WEAVER *rushes on, alarmed.)*

WEAVER: The Board is panicking!

SANDERS: What?

WEAVER: The entire Board. Owens' nose was right!

OWENS: You were there?

WEAVER: I could see through the glass wall of the conference room. The table was covered in documents. Stacks and reams. Board members standing and stomping and yelling—

SANDERS: Our Board—

WEAVER: One guy throws his suit jacket. Another cries tears on his tie clip.

LANDRY: *(To* OWENS:) They *are* panicking!

WEAVER: Legal pads fly. Someone kicks an attaché case and our annual report scatters in the air, columns and columns of figures. Assets and debits and cash flow and dividends and depreciations and tax liabilities all gripping the page in terror as the sheets zig and zag and turn upside down, carpeting where the ceiling should be! The Chairman, though—the Chairman stands still in the middle, arms crossed, staring out, silent amid the thumping and crashing. His clear blue eyes…like sea ice.

(Quick blackout)

Scene
"Stocks Fall"

(LANDRY, OWENS, SANDERS, *and* WEAVER.)

WEAVER: Our stock price—

OWENS: Dammit!

SANDERS: It's plummeting further!

LANDRY: Our market cap—

WEAVER: Is market capsizing!

OWENS: The exchanges have learned the truth about us.

LANDRY: Somebody leaked.

SANDERS: Leaked like Jesus on the cross!

WEAVER: The brokers all know.

OWENS: The business writers—

LANDRY: Even their pets are shorting us.

SANDERS: We need to sell our shares.

LANDRY: Never!

OWENS: Before they're worthless!

LANDRY: Fools! If we sell, we kill the company ourselves. We put a pillow on its face and push down till the kicking stops. No! This is what we're here to *stop*. All of us! You, me, and the receptionists who bring their lunch in *bags*.

WEAVER: We gotta fight this.

LANDRY: Failure is not acceptable.

SANDERS: Even a little of it?

LANDRY: No!

WEAVER: (*With a sudden big idea*) A proposal!

SANDERS: What?

WEAVER: A proposal!

LANDRY: Yes!

WEAVER: This crisis is a chance to prove ourselves to the Chairman—

LANDRY: *We* solve the crisis.

WEAVER: With a proposal.

LANDRY: A plan to save this company.

OWENS: He hasn't asked us.

WEAVER: Coward!

LANDRY: The stock plunge has cracked open—

WEAVER: A crevice of chance!

LANDRY: We gotta charge through it like the Chairman did when he started this place.

WEAVER: It's what made him.

LANDRY: It'll make *us*.

WEAVER: Promotions.

SANDERS: Raises.

LANDRY: Valets parking our cars.

OWENS: *(Coming around to idea)* And looking in our glove compartment!

SANDERS: *(Coming around)* Yes!

WEAVER: The four of us together.

OWENS: As a team.

LANDRY: We work all day and through the night.

OWENS: We'll show him enterprise.

LANDRY: Enterprise!

WEAVER: No laziness!

LANDRY: Laziness is for heiresses.

OWENS: Heiresses on divans.

SANDERS: We start *now*.

WEAVER: To work!

LANDRY, OWENS, SANDERS, & WEAVER: *(Together)* *To work!*

(They each break for a corner of the stage, then all begin pacing in a kind of choreographed way.)

WEAVER: We need ideas.

LANDRY: Breakthroughs.

OWENS: New perspectives.

WEAVER: Fresh angles.

SANDERS: A new logo.

LANDRY: Yes!

OWENS: On our business cards.

WEAVER: Our letterhead.

LANDRY: On buildings across the skyline.

OWENS: Something modern.

SANDERS: Cutting edge.

LANDRY: That says "today".

SANDERS: *(Improving the idea)* "Tomorrow"!

LANDRY: Right!

SANDERS: That says, "We'll get to it *tomorrow*."

OWENS: No—that change is cosmetic.

WEAVER: We need core changes.

OWENS: A restructure.

WEAVER: A whole new shape. A shape previously unknown to geometry. One to give Euclid a migraine!

OWENS: We must reject the past, but learn from it.

SANDERS: Where others went wrong.

WEAVER: How they thought—

LANDRY: Dreamed—

SANDERS: But screwed up.

OWENS: We need changes in accounting.

WEAVER: Work flow.

SANDERS: New logistics.

LANDRY: New protocols.

OWENS: We must not be out-protocolled!

WEAVER: The history of business is littered with the ruins of companies that got out-protocolled.

SANDERS: Burned-out factories.

OWENS: Empty airline hangers.

LANDRY: Rusting ocean liners.

WEAVER: Law firms covered in graffiti and blood.

(Quick blackout)

Scene
"Bestsellers"

(WEAVER and OWENS, urgently re proposal. WEAVER holds a couple books.)

OWENS: You have?!

WEAVER: Read 'em all. All the bestsellers by great business leaders—

OWENS: That's a lot.

WEAVER: I've wanted every speck of knowledge from the people on those covers.

OWENS: Yes!

WEAVER: Their ideas, Owens. We can use them in our proposal! Successful businesses are *ideas*. Are creativity. Sure, I could do ceramics. That's creativity too. Colorful tiles for this office—

OWENS: But it's *business* for us.

WEAVER: After we save this place, I'll write my own memoir.

OWENS: I'll buy it!

WEAVER: In airports. Waving it at stewardesses as you board the plane.

OWENS: People will quote you at graduations.

WEAVER: Wise valedictorians in black robes.

OWENS: What have you learned that can help us?

WEAVER: Their stratagems.

OWENS: You mean "strategies"?

WEAVER: Strata-*gems*. Because they're gems of strategy.

OWENS: Genius!

WEAVER: These authors worked in business for years.

OWENS: They've got resumés.

WEAVER: Thick ones with bullet points. There's no problem they haven't faced.

OWENS: What do they say about debt?

WEAVER: Just a number.

OWENS: The laws?

WEAVER: Obey the good ones.

OWENS: Lawyers?

WEAVER: Bright people with nice cufflinks.

OWENS: Nuclear power stocks?

WEAVER: Sell 'em—it's eve for the atom.

OWENS: The penguin?

WEAVER: A bird that must be some sort of metaphor.

(SANDERS *rushes on.* SANDERS *is holding up a yellow highlighter in each hand, showing them to* WEAVER.)

SANDERS: Weaver, Weaver—we can use these!

WEAVER: No! They're antiques!

SANDERS: These are *the wands of importance.* Any words they touch become extra significant.

WEAVER: *Algorithms*, Sanders. Those are the tools we need. *(Re highlighters)* Not those. New equations. Math of the finest gossamer that will shape this economy's future.

SANDERS: Impossible.

WEAVER: Failure-ist!

SANDERS: No!

WEAVER: That's giving failure a big wet kiss. That's stroking the nipple of failure's big, bared, bulbous breast.

SANDERS: That's alliterative.

WEAVER: I don't care what country it's from, we're saving this company!

(Quick blackout)

Scene
"Wrong Number"

(LANDRY *onstage, isolated in a spotlight. He holds up his cellphone and taps it to make call. We hear ringing and then lights up on* SANDERS *across the stage. He pulls out his ringing phone and answers.)*

SANDERS: Hello?

LANDRY: *(Mistakenly thinking he's talking to* OWENS*)* Owens, it's Landry.

*(*LANDRY *takes phone away from his ear, as he looks around to see that he's not being watched.)*

SANDERS: No, it's Sanders.

*(*LANDRY *has phone back to his ear, having not heard* SANDERS*.)*

LANDRY: Owens, I've got news. News that could really affect the proposal.

SANDERS: *(Trying to correct)* No, this is—

LANDRY: Just listen!

*(*SANDERS*, confused by the call, does not reply.)*

LANDRY: Owens, are you there?

SANDERS: *(Thinking fast and disguising his voice)* Yeah, yeah.

LANDRY: I've heard a rumor from upstairs. From the big offices. The Chairman *does not like Weaver.*

SANDERS: No?

LANDRY: Not. At. All.

SANDERS: Why not?

LANDRY: Sources only have guesses. *Keep these to yourself.*

SANDERS: Okay.

LANDRY: Could be his astrological sign. You follow astrology, Owens?

SANDERS: Nope.

LANDRY: It's like astronomy but for girls. Maybe his politics—it's okay to care about other people, but everything in moderation.

SANDERS: Right.

LANDRY: We need to find out the Chairman's reason.

SANDERS: Will do.

LANDRY: You okay, Owens?

SANDERS: Yeah.

LANDRY: You sound kind of strange today. Like a throat infection. Be careful of bacteria, Owens. Bacteria is everywhere. Unlike you and me, some people don't wipe their behind properly. They might try, but their aim is off. Can't blame 'em—it's hard see back there. Unless you wipe in a mirror. I do that once a week as a precaution. If your throat is infected from bacteria, it's probably not mine.

SANDERS: Good.

LANDRY: I'd feel like hell, Owens, if you were sick from a wiping blunder on my part.

(Quick blackout)

Scene
"Chairman Rumor"

(SANDERS *and* WEAVER*)*

SANDERS: *(urgently)* Why does the Chairman hate you?

WEAVER: What?

SANDERS: I need to know—*now!*

WEAVER: The Chairman barely knows me —

SANDERS: The rumors are everywhere.

WEAVER: Impossible!

SANDERS: You're not taking us all down with you!

WEAVER: I only met him once before today. At the big conference. His after-shave smelled like ocean and fortitude.

SANDERS: But the rumors—

WEAVER: They're false.

SANDERS: They better be!

WEAVER: People spread rumors, Sanders. It's human nature. We've got bad instincts. Can't give in to them! Give in to instincts and civilization collapses. Ever seen civilization collapse?

SANDERS: No.

WEAVER: It's gunfire and looted museums and negative attitude.

SANDERS: Damn.

WEAVER: If you believe what they say about me, I'll have to believe what they say about *you*.

SANDERS: *Me*?

WEAVER: Don't make me believe those things, Sanders.

SANDERS: But—

WEAVER: Don't make me believe....

(Quick blackout)

Scene
"Different Suit"

(LANDRY, OWENS, and WEAVER. SANDERS enters. He is now wearing a slightly different suit from the one he has been wearing—for costume-change simplicity, it could just be a new suit jacket, one with different lapels. The others notice this, but do not yet say anything about it. SANDERS notes that the others are looking at him, but tries to ignore them by looking at the contents of his folder. The others continue to look at him. Then OWENS speaks.)

OWENS: *(To SANDERS)* You're wearing a different suit.

SANDERS: *(Looking up as if he hasn't heard)* Hmmm?

WEAVER: You're wearing a different suit.

LANDRY: The lapels are different.

OWENS: Wider.

SANDERS: *(Innocently)* Are they?

LANDRY: It's a different suit from earlier today.

SANDERS: *(Brushing it off)* Oh, I guess so. Yes.

(Pause)

OWENS: What's… what's going on?

SANDERS: *(Low-grade defensively)* What's going on?

LANDRY: Yes.

SANDERS: Strategy meeting for our big proposal.

WEAVER: What's going on with the suit?

SANDERS: You like it?

LANDRY, OWENS, AND WEAVER: *(Together)* No.

SANDERS: What do we need to do first?

LANDRY: You're interviewing somewhere else.

OWENS: Another company.

SANDERS: It's just a different suit.

WEAVER: What was wrong with your old one?

SANDERS: *(Now nervous)* Bad…pockets.

(Pause)

LANDRY: It looks like the suits people wear across town.

OWENS: He wants to work for them.

SANDERS: I'm working with you guys.

WEAVER: So you got a different suit.

SANDERS: With better pockets, yes.

(Pause)

LANDRY: No wonder his proposal ideas have been so weak.

SANDERS: No, they haven't.

WEAVER: He's saving his good ideas for across town.

LANDRY: Maybe he's already given them those.

SANDERS: Hey—

LANDRY: To get in good.

OWENS: Then bought the suit at lunch.

WEAVER: He's spying!

SANDERS: Now wait—

WEAVER: Stealing our ideas and passing them along. *(To* SANDERS*)* What are they giving you?! Money? Sex? Some kind of great drug that makes your eyes see everything in plaid?!

SANDERS: No!

WEAVER: You know what happens to spies on this team?

*(*SANDERS *makes a "doesn't know" gesture.)*

WEAVER: *(To* LANDRY *and* OWENS*)* Tell him!

*(*LANDRY *and* WEAVER *look at each other, not knowing.)*

WEAVER: *(To* SANDERS*)* We'll… *think of something!* And it's going to be bad, oh yeah. It's going to be painful and complicated. The Spanish Inquisition will be really jealous. They'll want it too, but we'll *patent* it. Send it to the *patent office,* where they'll stamp it and applaud, 'cause they've never seen such a vicious thing. The whole patent office standing and clapping, then leaving early 'cause no patent's going to top that today, no sir, no sir, no m'am! Go hit the bars instead. All the good patent-office bars. Then the Spanish

Inquisition calls and asks to use it, but we're "No!"
So they rip their ruff collars in frustration and start
cursing in elaborate Spanish tenses, tenses that sound
contradictory when used together but are the height of
Spanish invective. Because of *you!*

OWENS: Your treachery!

LANDRY: Your lies!

WEAVER: Your new single-breasted splendor!

*(SANDERS suddenly lurches away and rushes to the
downstage "window.")*

SANDERS: Stay back! I could do it—break the glass and
hurl myself out!

WEAVER: Sanders!

SANDERS: Into the cold, cold air—

OWENS: Away from the window!

SANDERS: Hover a second, then start my fall!

WEAVER: He's lost it.

SANDERS: Slowly at first, then picking up speed. Suit
flapping—

LANDRY: Sanders!

SANDERS: Accelerating at 9.8 meters-per-second-
squared!

OWENS: Don't kill yourself in metric!

SANDERS: The floors zipping past me, the concrete
below—

LANDRY: You can't!

SANDERS: Plunging faster and faster. Leaving all this
behind!

OWENS: Not worth it!

SANDERS: The last hundred feet, then *splat!*

(LANDRY, OWENS, *and* WEAVER *all recoil, as if they've just witnessed the actual splat.*)

SANDERS: Hit the sidewalk and explode! A huge wet thump as my insides blast through my skin! Pieces of me fly everywhere. Bones, muscles. A kidney smacks a banker, a femur pierces the window of a menswear shop, bone marrow landing on a table of silk ties. People on the street flee, dropping bags and briefcases, losing hats and takeout lunches, running from the lump of muck and wingtips that used to be *me*!

LANDRY: There are things to live for!

SANDERS: I'm doing it!

OWENS: Please!

SANDERS: To show you all!

LANDRY: *Sanders!*

SANDERS: Now!

WEAVER: Stop!

SANDERS: *Nowwwwww!!*

(*Quick blackout*)

Scene
"Apologies"

(LANDRY, OWENS, *and* WEAVER *all together. They look at each other guiltily. Then* SANDERS *enters.* SANDERS *did not jump. A pause, everyone uncomfortable. Then* OWENS *speaks.*)

OWENS: We're sorry.

WEAVER: We're sorry we thought you were a spy.

(*Pause*)

LANDRY: We're sorry about your new suit.

WEAVER: What we said.

OWENS: It's a nice suit.

LANDRY: A new suit doesn't make someone a spy.

WEAVER: I want a suit like that someday.

OWENS: *(Re WEAVER)* He'd look good in it.

LANDRY: He would.

SANDERS: Thank you for grabbing me and pulling me back.

WEAVER: If you had jumped—

OWENS: Boy—

LANDRY: If you had died—

WEAVER: The whole office would've been like—

OWENS: I know—

WEAVER: Like, "Which one was he?"

LANDRY: Jumping—

WEAVER: Not worth it.

OWENS: No way.

LANDRY: Never.

OWENS: Unless he jumped and suddenly learned he could fly.

WEAVER: *(To SANDERS)* We're glad you're still here.

LANDRY: *(To SANDERS)* That you're back.

WEAVER: If you died, there'd be a funeral.

LANDRY: Lots of people would think they could make it.

WEAVER: People would get up and talk about you.

OWENS: Tell anecdotes.

LANDRY: Then reflect on their own lives.

OWENS: Giving thanks they weren't you—

LANDRY: Shoveled together in that coffin.

WEAVER: They'd vow to live better.

OWENS: To stop and smell the roses.

LANDRY: Maybe snap a few off to smell on the way home.

WEAVER: No one would notice.

LANDRY: Plenty of roses on that lady's bush.

OWENS: Then the hearse would take you away.

WEAVER: Lumbering down the road.

OWENS: Through stoplights.

LANDRY: And in through the cemetery gates.

WEAVER: The trees and graves and chiseled headstones.

LANDRY: And ghosts!

OWENS: Everywhere around.

WEAVER: Their cold presence brushing the backs of our necks.

LANDRY: Suicides like you—

WEAVER: Cursed to haunt this world forever.

OWENS: Rattling chains.

WEAVER: Trapped for eternity.

LANDRY: No heaven for them.

WEAVER: Just the gravestones.

OWENS: And fog.

WEAVER: And moldering bones.

OWENS: It's only heaven for the worms.

(Quick blackout)

Scene
"Conference Call"

(In the dark, the sound of conference call machinery—clicks, beeps, and quick hint of hold music. Then lights up on WEAVER *with conference call unit. Others characters can just be voices, or stand with phones in isolated lights.)*

WEAVER: Is everybody there? Everyone on the line for this proposal conference call?

SANDERS: I'm downstairs with the logistics experts.

OWENS: I'm in the A/V room looking at presentation tech.

WEAVER: Landry, you in accounting? *(Pause)* Landry? *(Pause)* Where's Landry?

SANDERS: He knows about it.

WEAVER: Dammit—we don't have time for—

*(*WEAVER *is interrupted by dial tone of lost connections. Then there's beeping and brief snatches of hold music again as connection between everyone is reestablished.)*

OWENS: You guys there?

SANDERS: I'm back.

WEAVER: Someone find Landry.

LANDRY: I'm here.

WEAVER: Okay then, status reports!

OWENS: Our proposal outline.

LANDRY: Finished.

SANDERS: Overall strategy formulated.

WEAVER: Potential ramifications?

LANDRY: Laid out.

WEAVER: Unintended consequences?

OWENS: All considered.

WEAVER: If our proposal offends the public, there'll be protests in the streets, people shouting and waving clever placards.

OWENS: Who's our external spokesman?

SANDERS: Owens.

LANDRY: Practice your smile, Owens, and helpful similes.

WEAVER: What about our stock-price forecast?

OWENS: Solid.

SANDERS: Our plan builds back market confidence.

LANDRY: Investor faith.

OWENS: Our stock price will soar.

SANDERS: High.

LANDRY: Higher than a giraffe's best boner!

WEAVER: Excellent. Now let's—

(The connections are suddenly lost again. Some beeps then a shift to some Haydn playing as hold music.)

WEAVER: Owens? Sanders? *(Notices music)* What is this, Haydn? Goddammit, I told that phone company *no Haydn!*

(Quick blackout)

Scene
"Poor"

(SANDERS and OWENS, SANDERS distracted.)

OWENS: Something the matter?

SANDERS: *(Bursting out)* I don't want to be poor!

OWENS: *(Trying to calm him down)* Sanders—

SANDERS: I haven't worked this hard to end up broke! If we lose this, that's what we'll be. We'll never be hired again. My savings will drain down till there's nothing, and then I'm *poor*! I'll be begging on street corners, fighting off the other beggars. My face will grow saggy and rough, my hair unkempt. *Unkempt*! I'll end up in a soup kitchen. People will ladle me food and give me *encouraging smiles*. I'll wander the city with nothing to do, bending down to pick up mildly interesting objects. I'll see somebody's baby and weep, thinking of my own lost promise. A wee baby in a stroller sucking on a pacifier thinking it's its mama's boob. What an idiot! *(Gesturing)* There's no boob there! But with its whole life ahead of it. Not *busted* like me, standing on a traffic median with my cardboard sign. Like they care, as they lock their car doors. That I used to be just like them. Oh, cruel shoulder of fate!

OWENS: *(Correcting)* Hand of fate.

SANDERS: *(Making frustrated correction)* Hand!

(Quick blackout)

Scene
"Choosing Sides"

(LANDRY, OWENS, SANDERS, and LANDRY each hold a copy of the proposal. They all turn slowly through the first several pages, turning each page in unison. Then—)

LANDRY, OWENS, SANDERS, & WEAVER: *(Together)* It's crap!!!

OWENS: All our work but the proposal's garbage!

WEAVER: It's too long.

LANDRY: Too complicated.

OWENS: Who added the footnotes?!

SANDERS: *(Defending himself)* People *love* footnotes.

LANDRY: We worked like hell and now it's—

OWENS: Cat vomit.

WEAVER: Laced with —

LANDRY & WEAVER: *The fur of ineptitude!*

SANDERS: *(Panicking)* Oh, jeez, oh jeez—

LANDRY: The Chairman will laugh in our faces.

OWENS: Then fire us all!

SANDERS: There'll be nothing left to fire us *from*!

WEAVER: We have to try again.

OWENS: Trash it—

SANDERS: And start over!

LANDRY: *(Pointing at* WEAVER*)* Not with him!

WEAVER: *(Pointing at* OWENS*)* Not with *him*!

SANDERS: We can do it!

WEAVER: Owens' ideas were lameness.

LANDRY: *(Re* OWENS's *ideas)* No—

WEAVER: Lameness wrapped in fiasco.

LANDRY: *(Pointing at* OWENS*)* I'll do it with him.

OWENS: *(Pointing at* WEAVER*)* I'll do it with *him*.

SANDERS: We all do it together!

WEAVER: No more together! *(At* LANDRY *)* You and me as a pair—we'll save us.

LANDRY: *(Pointing at* OWENS*)* I'm gonna work with Owens.

OWENS: *(at* WEAVER*)* No, with me!

LANDRY: *(at* OWENS *)* Let's save this company.

OWENS: *(To* WEAVER*)* Teammates!

SANDERS: We're *all* a team.

OWENS: *(at* WEAVER*)* It's gotta be done by the morning.

WEAVER: *(at* LANDRY*)*: First thing!

OWENS: *(at* WEAVER *re* LANDRY*)* He can't be trusted.

WEAVER: *(at* LANDRY *re* OWENS*)* He'll screw up.

LANDRY: *(at* OWENS *re* WEAVER*)* He smokes—

OWENS: *(at* WEAVER *re* LANDRY*)* He drinks—

LANDRY: *(at* OWENS *re* WEAVER*)* He reads Victorian literature.

OWENS: *(at* WEAVER *)* I'll untap your potential.

LANDRY: *(Pleading to be partners) Owens.*

OWENS: Potential spraying *everywhere*!

WEAVER: *(at* LANDRY*)* We leave 'em behind.

LANDRY: *(at* OWENS*)* Leave *them* behind!

OWENS: *(at* WEAVER*)* They'll teach us in business schools.

WEAVER: *(at* LANDRY*)* In history books.

LANDRY: *(at* OWENS*)* In poems.

SANDERS: Poems?

LANDRY: They're sentiment plus rhyme!

WEAVER: *(To* LANDRY*)* We can beat these guys.

SANDERS: What about me?!

(They all stop and look at SANDERS. *Beat. Then jump back into the argument.)*

WEAVER: *(at* LANDRY*)* I'll buy you pornography.

OWENS: *(at* WEAVER*)* Useless!

WEAVER: Pornography rich in detail!

LANDRY: *(at* OWENS *)* Use my desk.

WEAVER: *(at* LANDRY *)* My phone.

OWENS: *(at* WEAVER*)* My family photos.

LANDRY: *(at* OWENS *)* My kids have prettier faces.

WEAVER: *(at* LANDRY *)* Better smiles.

OWENS: *(at* WEAVER*)* Less curved spines.

LANDRY: *(at* OWENS *)* I'll give you my tie.

WEAVER: *(at* LANDRY*)* My watch—

LANDRY: *(at* OWENS *)* My aura.

SANDERS: He has no aura.

LANDRY: I got a top-shelf aura!

OWENS: *(To* LANDRY*)* Your aura plus cash.

LANDRY: Deal!

(A beat as LANDRY *and* OWENS *look at each other with clarity and determination, while* SANDERS *and* WEAVER *look on in shock and disappointment and the realization that they are stuck with each other. Then quick blackout.)*

Scene
"New Team: Landry and Owens"

*(*LANDRY *and* OWENS, *together as new team.)*

OWENS: I'm glad we're partners.

LANDRY: You wanted Weaver first.

OWENS: That's history, like the Roosevelts or witch burning. Only the future matters now. The future, a place with light sabers and light...catapults.

LANDRY: What if we *do* find a witch? What's the policy?

OWENS: *(Waving off distracting question)* There are no witches in this company.

LANDRY: That's an *assumption*. What's our current witch policy?

OWENS: *(Ignoring LANDRY's concern) The future*, Landry. We're here all night to finish our new proposal. You, me, *us*. "Nas" in Russian, "meita" in Finnish. The Finns would understand—a civilized people with bellies full of beer and reindeer. We can do it *together*, Landry. A team! Like left and right or carbon and monoxide!

(Quick pause as LANDRY and OWENS look at each other. Then quick blackout.)

Scene
"New Team: Sanders and Weaver"

(SANDERS and WEAVER, grudgingly new teammates. They're looking at documents for their new proposal. Then SANDERS looks up from his sheet.)

SANDERS: There's a mistake in Column Two.

WEAVER: *(Sharply)* I know.

(Quiet, as they look at their sheets.)

SANDERS: Sixteen (C) should be cut.

WEAVER: Already have.

(Quiet, as they look at their sheets.)

SANDERS: We should move up Section Five—

(WEAVER suddenly erupts.)

WEAVER: You mother-birthing son of an aunt-poking cousin's sister-cussing father's dog-kicking godchild's puking stepbrother of a foster delinquent's phlegm-snorting long-lost pity-adopted twin of a half-niece's semi-autistic au pair's bastard's twice-removed black-sheep nephew's eldest sibling's great-great-grand-trollop!!!

(Pause)

SANDERS: And we can flip Paragraphs Six and Seven.

WEAVER: We'll never win together.

SANDERS: We *can*.

WEAVER: We're going to be here all night with you dragging me down.

SANDERS: I'm sorry about my shortcomings.

(SANDERS *passes a piece of paper to* WEAVER.)

SANDERS: I wrote them up for you in a memo.

(WEAVER *inspects the memo.)*

WEAVER: *(Somewhat impressed)* This list of faults is quite well-organized.

SANDERS: Thank you.

WEAVER: *(Re memo)* What's "beguileful"? Is that like knavery?

SANDERS: Sorta.

WEAVER: It says here you're impatie— *(Starting the word "impatient")*

SANDERS: Yep!

WEAVER: And this one: "aulophobia."

SANDERS: Fear of flutes.

WEAVER: Like in a…symphony orchestra?

(WEAVER *makes a flute-playing gesture and sound and* SANDERS *covers his ears and looks hugely panicked. Quick blackout)*

Scene
"Arabic Numbers"

*(*LANDRY *and* OWENS.*)*

OWENS: *(Suggesting)* Or a new company slogan.

LANDRY: No! This is a business and we need a *business* answer.

OWENS: Something with numbers—

LANDRY: With numbers, dammit! Those numerals given to us by the Arabs. Don't let their clothing fool you—Arabs are *savvy*.

OWENS: But their sandals!

LANDRY: A race proud of their toes.

OWENS: They cover their women in sheets.

LANDRY: So they can sleep *anywhere*! The Arabs worship Allah.

OWENS: He's a big shot.

LANDRY: The biggest! You may speak Allah's name, but not graven his image. Engrave it and he'll smite us all.

OWENS: *(Worried)* Smite us?

LANDRY: Into smite nuggets!

OWENS: How does Allah compare to our God?

LANDRY: When they meet, our God covers his nuts.

(Quick blackout)

Scene
"Thesaurus"

(SANDERS *and* WEAVER. WEAVER *is holding up a thesaurus.*)

SANDERS: What's that?

WEAVER: A thesaurus. I found it on a secretary's desk.

SANDERS: What's it for?

WEAVER: Synonyms.

SANDERS: Like for synonym buns?

WEAVER: No, Sanders—*words*. A book full of different words that mean the same thing.

SANDERS: A book of redundancies?

WEAVER: All the best writers use one. Look at any book-jacket photo and there's the author with his thesaurus.

SANDERS: I write well already—

WEAVER: Not like you will with a thesaurus! Our sentences are going to shine! You like nuance?

SANDERS: Sure.

WEAVER: (*Waving book*) This is a nuance goldmine! When the Chairman reads our proposal he'll smile and nod at our vocab. Our *winning* vocab! (*Pause*) Let's look up "buttucks."

(*Quick blackout*)

Scene
"Evolution"

(LANDRY *and* OWENS, *working.*)

OWENS: Why are we here?

LANDRY: Sorry?

OWENS: Why are we here, any of us?

LANDRY: Need jobs.

OWENS: Evolution? We were apes once, you and me.

LANDRY: I don't remember that.

OWENS: Once upon a time.

LANDRY: No, I mean I'd remember that.

OWENS: Whoever started this planet put together
a business plan and started it and at some point in
evolution we were apes.

LANDRY: Glad I'm not an ape now.

OWENS: *(Looking on good side)* If you're an ape, no one
would expect you to keep appointments.

LANDRY: Would still hate it.

OWENS: Might be okay.

LANDRY: If I'm an ape, my credit-card interest rate is
high.

OWENS: Maybe.

LANDRY: Go to a concerto, they won't give you a
program.

OWENS: But it's classical.

LANDRY: If you're an ape, one day you're just walking
around doing errands and some guy sneaks up with
a *net* and puts you in a *circus.* You know how much I
hate calliope?

OWENS: I guess why we're here is a mystery. Or maybe
we're gods ourselves, but just don't realize it.

LANDRY: Like gods, but dim?

OWENS: We could be dim gods.

(A pause as they both pick their heads up and stare into space considering this idea. They start raising their hands to their chins to contemplate, but a quick blackout occurs just before their hands get there.)

Scene
"Hypnotized?"

(SANDERS and WEAVER looking at LANDRY and OWENS.)

WEAVER: *(To SANDERS)* They are.

LANDRY: No—

WEAVER: They *are*. *(Pause)* They're trying to use… psychology.

OWENS: Psychology?

SANDERS: *(To WEAVER)* You're right.

LANDRY: That's nonsense—

WEAVER: How they walked in here.

SANDERS: How they stood.

WEAVER: The handshakes.

SANDERS: The eye contact.

WEAVER: Unwavering.

SANDERS: How they spoke.

WEAVER: They used—

SANDERS & WEAVER: *(Together, pointing at LANDRY and OWENS) Reassuring tones!*

SANDERS: It was all psychology!

LANDRY: No!

OWENS: We're your friends—

LANDRY: *(Waving to outside the window)* We'd only use psychology out there.

OWENS: On the public.

SANDERS: *(More worried)* It could be worse—they may have hypnotized us!

LANDRY: *(Protesting)* Sanders—

SANDERS: We might be under their complete command.

WEAVER: Doing things to us.

SANDERS: Stealing our ideas.

WEAVER: Changing our perceptions—

SANDERS: Our personalities.

WEAVER: *(To* SANDERS*)* I might be you—

SANDERS: *(To* LANDRY *and* OWENS *re* WEAVER*)* I could be him!

WEAVER: *(Pointing at* SANDERS*)* Feeling his fears.

SANDERS: *(Angry, pointing at* WEAVER*)* Making his insights!

WEAVER: Hypnotized!

SANDERS: The ancient art of mind control invented by the alchemists.

OWENS: Who?

SANDERS: The alchemists, dammit! Men in conical hats, gatekeepers to the dark arts! *(Brief pause, then ominously to all)* Beware the man in a conical hat.

(Quick blackout)

Scene
"Counterintuitive"

*(*LANDRY *and* OWENS*)*

LANDRY & OWENS: *(Simultaneously, pointing at each other)* You're an idiot!

LANDRY: *(Mocking)* Psychology!

OWENS: It would have worked. The whole thing—

LANDRY: They saw right through it.

OWENS: We'll never win now!

LANDRY: We have to! If we lose, we're out on the street with the drunks and rats and tinkers. We're selling goatskins off carts—

OWENS: No! We'll find a new strategy.

LANDRY: Fast!

OWENS: Something counterintuitive!

LANDRY: Or counter-counter intuitive.

OWENS: Brilliant!

LANDRY: Unless they intuit that.

OWENS: No one intuits counter-counterintuition!

(Quick blackout)

Scene
"Not Hypnotized"

(SANDERS *and* WEAVER)

WEAVER: We're not hypnotized!

SANDERS: How do we know?!

WEAVER: It was too obvious—

SANDERS: What if the blatancy of their ploy was just a ruse to hide the fact they *did* hypnotize us? Look in my eyes!

WEAVER: No!

SANDERS: Are they glassy? Dilated?

WEAVER: I can't tell.

SANDERS: The control word—there's always a control word!

WEAVER: What?!

SANDERS: "Pollywog"!

WEAVER: Get a grip —

SANDERS: "Periwinkle"!

WEAVER: The stress is snapping you. Don't kill this team. *(Grabs* SANDERS *by the shoulders)* Don't dissolve on me, Sanders. Not now. It's no time for the nut house. Don't go there! The nut house is all linoleum and straitjackets and people teaching their genitals Welsh!

*(*WEAVER *exits angrily.* SANDERS *then notices that his shoe is untied and bends down to tie it. Then he pulls a handkerchief from his pocket and polishes the shoe. Then he starts admiring the reflection in the polished shoe.)*

SANDERS: Ah, reflection! *(A brief pause, then he addresses his reflection in his shoe.)*
Sanders, Sanders, in the shoe
Tell me please oh what to do.
Give some vision of our fate
Cough it up, expostulate!

All around is building fear,
Worry in this business sphere.
Panic travels through the air—
Dang it all, this laissez-faire!

How to stanch our stock price drop?
Could we do an asset swap?
If we tried to globalize,
Might that make our markets rise?

Do not let the brokers gape
As they hold the ticker tape.

Something—now!—to meet new goals,
Saving also both our souls.

(*Quick blackout*)

Scene
"Coffee Place"

(OWENS *and* WEAVER *meet accidently in the building's lobby coffee shop. Both are holding takeout coffee cups. The meeting is awkward.*)

WEAVER: Owens.

OWENS: Weaver.

(*Pause*)

WEAVER: Getting coffee from this lobby coffee place.

OWENS: Before it closes for the night.

WEAVER: Mine's a Sumatra blend.

(*Pause*)

OWENS: Used to come to here together.

WEAVER: Yep.

OWENS: Before the proposal.

(*Both sip awkwardly from their cups.*)

OWENS: Yours…you and Sanders's coming along?

(WEAVER *slurps loudly from his coffee to avoid the question. Then changes topic.*)

WEAVER: Your sister still drinking too much?

OWENS: Won't stop.

WEAVER: Sad.

OWENS: Yep.

WEAVER: Alcoholics tell good stories, though.
(Pause) You still get those nightmares where you're a shuttlecock?

OWENS: No. *(Pause)* How's that cat you got?

WEAVER: Ran away.

OWENS: Sorry to hear.

WEAVER: Maybe it found a better life.

OWENS: That can happen.

WEAVER: Some cats have aspirations.

(A pause as they each look at their coffees.)

WEAVER: Sometimes I would bring you up a coffee from this place.

OWENS: That was good of you.

WEAVER: The cup would start burning my fingers in the elevator. I would've shifted hands but I was holding my own cup in my other hand. So my fingers—they just had to burn while I watched the floor numbers go up.

OWENS: Sorry about that.

WEAVER: Ten, eleven, twelve. *(Pause)* Eighteen. *(Pause)* All the way up. Then you'd look really happy when I walked up to your desk and gave it to you.

OWENS: It's nice coffee.

WEAVER: Just stop everything you were doing.

(Long pause, then quick blackout.)

Scene
"Flashlights"

(The scene starts in the dark. Then, in the dark, a flashlight beam. It's LANDRY, though we can't see him, just the beam,

which seems to be searching for something. While LANDRY
*is on one side of the stage, we see another flashlight beam
on the other side. Though we can't clearly see him, it's*
SANDERS, *also looking for something. A few moments of just
the flashlight beams, then the two see each other, illuminated
only by their flashlight beams.)*

SANDERS: Landry.

LANDRY: Sanders.

(Pause)

SANDERS: *(Suspiciously)* How you doing?

LANDRY: *(Suspiciously)* Okay. And how…how is your
night going?

SANDERS: My night is…fine.

LANDRY: What are you looking for?

SANDERS: Nightcrawlers.

LANDRY: Here in the conference room?

SANDERS: Might go…fishing soon. What are *you* doing
here?

LANDRY: Making sure the lights were all off.

SANDERS: Conservation.

LANDRY: It's the only responsible future we have.

(Pause)

SANDERS: You're not looking for me and Weaver's
proposal?

LANDRY: Your proposal? Why would I want to steal an
inferior proposal? Maybe you're looking for me and
Owens's.

SANDERS: I'm looking for *bait.*

(A noise from off-stage, SANDERS *suddenly turning and
aiming his flashlight at it.)*

SANDERS: What was that?!

(LANDRY *aims his flashlight the same direction.*)

LANDRY: *(With relief)* Just the immigrant cleaning guy.

SANDERS: He vacuums quite well.

LANDRY: They vacuum from birth in that country.

(Quick blackout)

Scene
"Generals"

(SANDERS *and* WEAVER)

SANDERS: *(Urgently)* How did the generals do it?!

WEAVER: What?

SANDERS: The generals who won World War Two.

WEAVER: They had tanks and carpet bombing—

SANDERS: How did they do it as *men*? As mortals who beat back a vast enemy.

WEAVER: Our generals had huge flotillas—

SANDERS: No! No, what did they have here?! *(Pounds his chest)* In here, coursing through their ventricles?!

WEAVER: That's blood—

SANDERS: No! Something else! They had what we need. That something *else* that inspired soldiers to storm beaches and charge machine-gun nests while the generals watched from the back around table maps drinking black coffee. *What was it?!* Something *special*. Transcendence. Where do we find it? Who do we appease? What must we sacrifice to get it?

WEAVER: A beast!

SANDERS: A beast! Of course! That's what they're *here* for!

WEAVER: Their fur—

SANDERS: Their tails—

WEAVER: God *made* them for sacrifice!

SANDERS: Their complete inability to plead their way out of it.

WEAVER: A sacrifice!

SANDERS: Tonight.

WEAVER: *Tonight.*

(Quick blackout)

Scene
"Binoculars 1"

(LANDRY and OWENS. LANDRY is looking out the window with binoculars, which he does throughout the scene.)

OWENS: Naked.

LANDRY: Huh?

OWENS: Naked people not knowing they're being watched.

LANDRY: No.

OWENS: Body parts flopping. Special areas lathered in soap.

LANDRY: *(Re his view through the binoculars)* It's an office building.

OWENS: Naked executives.

LANDRY: A *glass* office building. A glass building reflecting *this* building. I can see into our offices using it as a mirror. Weaver's office. Sanders'. The Chairman's floor upstairs.

OWENS: To see what they're doing.

LANDRY: Some would call this spying. Perhaps a gross invasion of privacy or some other term salted with moralizing.

OWENS: *(Enthusiastic)* Spying!

LANDRY: A great calling. Many spies gave their life for it. Not the best spies—the best spies never get caught. But noble, second-tier spies standing in front of firing squads in foreign countries, places with better cafés than us, but whose mysteries can only be deduced via the microdot.

OWENS: *(Re binoculars)* We can watch their faces.

LANDRY: Read their body language. Like a book. Like one of the great novels.

OWENS: Which one?

LANDRY: One with a tragic heroine. Ever met a tragic heroine?

OWENS: Nope.

LANDRY: They smell like perfume and oncoming locomotive.

(Quick blackout)

Scene
"The Sacrifice"

(SANDERS and WEAVER enter. They have blood on their hands from the sacrifice and seem rather disturbed. They inspect their hands a bit, then speak.)

WEAVER: That didn't go so well.

SANDERS: There was a lot of wiggling.

WEAVER: More than you'd think.

(Pause)

SANDERS: Were we supposed to incant supplications during that?

(WEAVER *reacts in frustration because they forgot. Then regathers himself.*)

WEAVER: Did you put the knife back in the office kitchen?

SANDERS: Yes.

WEAVER: People need it for the birthday cakes.

(SANDERS *suddenly looks around nervously and suspiciously.*)

WEAVER: What?

SANDERS: I feel like I'm being watched.

WEAVER: No one here but us.

SANDERS: I know—

WEAVER: *(Indicating)* No cameras anywhere.

SANDERS: I feel it.

WEAVER: You're being paranoid.

SANDERS: In the air.

WEAVER: *(Re work)* Focus!

SANDERS: It's *something.*

WEAVER: Focus on the work.

SANDERS: I'm trying.

WEAVER: No distraction. Distraction killed all the great empires.

SANDERS: The Romans?

WEAVER: Distracted.

SANDERS: Austro-Hungarians?

WEAVER: Day-dreamed.

SANDERS: The Ottomans?

WEAVER: Wandering minds. The Ottomans screwed up big-time! They could've had it all. We'd be speaking Ottoman today. Looking at each other and making deep guttural sounds.

SANDERS: Even movie stars?

WEAVER: Would be Ottomans. Living in Hollywood minarets.

SANDERS: This office?

WEAVER: All of us. Wearing elaborate headdresses and putting cumin on our privates.

(Quick blackout)

Scene
"Binoculars 2"

(OWENS and LANDRY. LANDRY is using the binoculars again. OWENS is also squinting out the window trying to see.)

OWENS: What do you see on the Chairman's floor now?

LANDRY: Nothing. It's black.

OWENS: Dammit.

LANDRY: Lights on before, but none now.

OWENS: Smart bosses know it's best to work in the dark. What about Weaver and Sanders' office?

LANDRY: *(Shifting his binoculars)* Movements and paper.

OWENS: Yeah?

LANDRY: There was pacing earlier.

OWENS: And arguments?

LANDRY: And finger pointing.

OWENS: They're falling apart.

LANDRY: Now they're just sitting. Sitting and looking sad.

OWENS: Like mopers.

LANDRY: Like ne'er-do-wells.

OWENS: *Ne'er!*

LANDRY: They don't have it. They're weaklings. You know what's wrong with weaklings? They *like* it. Inside, they actually like it. They want someone standing over them about to bring the broadsword down. But we still gotta learn their secrets. Time is running down.

OWENS: The hours—

LANDRY: The minutes—

OWENS: The seconds.

LANDRY: Tick.

OWENS: Tock.

LANDRY: Tick.

OWENS: Tock.

LANDRY: Tick.

(No response from OWENS, *who's distracted looking out window. Pause, then…)*

LANDRY: *Tock, Owens, tock!*

(Quick blackout)

Scene
"Figments"

*(*WEAVER *and* SANDERS*)*

WEAVER: You still feel watched?

SANDERS: Nope.

WEAVER: Okay.

SANDERS: A figment of my imagination.

WEAVER: *(Dismissively)* Figments.

SANDERS: You get 'em?

WEAVER: Figments?

SANDERS: Right.

WEAVER: Christ, no.

SANDERS: I get 'em. Little figments. But not now. *(Re proposal)* Right now my mind's on this.

WEAVER: Good!

SANDERS: On every period and comma.

WEAVER: Yes!

SANDERS: Every semi-colon.

WEAVER: Perfect!

SANDERS: Every ellipsis.

WEAVER: What's an ellipsis?

SANDERS: It's when....

(Long beat. Then quick blackout.)

Scene
"Binoculars 3"

(LANDRY and OWENS. OWENS is now holding binoculars and looking out with them.)

LANDRY: *(Re binoculars)* Those are mine!

OWENS: One minute—

LANDRY: Owens!

OWENS: Binoculars make everything closer.

LANDRY: Give them back—

OWENS: These are amazing!

LANDRY: Thank Galileo.

OWENS: Galileo?

LANDRY: He put lenses in front of each other we could see truths far, far in the distance.

OWENS: So we could see *all*.

LANDRY: See all for *ourselves*. Without the Church and Holy See. The Pope was furious—a greater fury than Earth had ever known. So the Pope killed him. With his own bejeweled hands, fingernails digging into Galileo's neck. Long, dirty fingernails because hygiene then was *crap*. You'd smash rats with your bare hands, then go pick your best friend's nose. The Pope too, and now he's strangling Galileo! Pushing his fingers way in, and Galileo's eyes are bulging and he's gurgling and foaming and trying to beg and say equations, and the Pope is like, "Take that, Mister Italian Genius!" And then Galileo is dead! The Pope gives him a kick to be sure, a huge kick with his red slipper, and stands up and straightens his toque and issues an encyclical, a really firm encyclical in Latin. Because Latin used to be *excellent!*

(*Quick blackout*)

Scene
"Late-Night Fatigue"

(SANDERS *and* WEAVER, *very late at night.*)

WEAVER: Late.

SANDERS: Late.

WEAVER: So dark out there.

SANDERS: Outside the office.

WEAVER: Still at work.

SANDERS: Working.

WEAVER: Thinking.

SANDERS: Crossing things out.

(Pause)

WEAVER: What's an idea?

SANDERS: Huh?

WEAVER: What's an idea? What *is* it? *(Waves his hands in the air)* Can't hold it. Can't...stick your finger in it.

SANDERS: Nope.

WEAVER: Can't stick your finger way inside it and see how good it feels.

SANDERS: They're weird.

WEAVER: Yep.

SANDERS: Ideas... *(Waves hands)* ...don't poop.

WEAVER: Nope.

SANDERS: An idea can be shitty, but it does not itself poop.

WEAVER: I poop.

SANDERS: You're not an idea.

WEAVER: Sometimes I poop here in the office restroom.

SANDERS: I don't.

WEAVER: No?

SANDERS: Never at the office. Hold it in.

WEAVER: Why?

SANDERS: Someone comes in the office bathroom while you're....

WEAVER: Yeah?

SANDERS: They get a whiff, hear your splashes…now they *know* you.

WEAVER: Huh?

SANDERS: And never look at you the same way again.

WEAVER: But—

SANDERS: They don't. Might seem like they do, but inside… *(Points to his head)* …inside they're always hearing your splashes.

(No reply from WEAVER. Quiet for a moment.)

WEAVER: Dark.

SANDERS: Dark.

WEAVER: You ever wonder….

SANDERS: Huh?

WEAVER: Ever wonder about…..

SANDERS: Yeah?

WEAVER: The letter "j."

SANDERS: Uhm…

WEAVER: People don't talk about it much.

SANDERS: I guess.

WEAVER: "Cross your t's and dot your i's." Well, you can dot a "j" too, but no one gives a damn about that.

SANDERS: I suppose.

WEAVER: Everything else needs to be absolutely perfect, but your j's—

(WEAVER waves his hand in a "who cares" gesture. Then it's quiet again for a moment until SANDERS speaks.)

SANDERS: Some people think the Earth is hollow.

WEAVER: Really?

SANDERS: And that there's a whole other population of humans living in the inside of it.

WEAVER: With houses?

SANDERS: Yep.

WEAVER: And golf courses?

SANDERS: They say.

WEAVER: *(Sort of to himself)* I wonder what a tee time costs.

(A longer pause. Then WEAVER *looks suspiciously at* SANDERS.*)*

WEAVER: You're thinking about my splashes.

(Quick blackout)

Scene
"The Imp"

*(*LANDRY *and* OWENS. *Night.* OWENS *holds a coffee mug,* LANDRY *holds some papers.)*

LANDRY: *(Irritated)* Back from the microwave again.

OWENS: *(Re mug)* I don't like lukewarm.

LANDRY: I don't like luke-*focus. (Waving files)* Like— what are these?!

OWENS: Our files.

LANDRY: Where'd I find them?

OWENS: Your desk?

LANDRY: The hallway!

OWENS: What?!

LANDRY: You left them there!

OWENS: No.

LANDRY: All our ideas!

OWENS: They've never left my hands or desk—

LANDRY: Our sheafs!

OWENS: It wasn't me!

LANDRY: This is where disaster comes from! From lack of attention! This is what happens when your brain turns casual, puts on shorts, and invites neighbors in for Old Fashioneds.

OWENS: I swear I didn't leave them there.

LANDRY: Look at them!

OWENS: Somebody took them.

LANDRY: Who?

OWENS: Sanders.

LANDRY: No—

OWENS: Weaver—

LANDRY: Never.

OWENS: An imp.

LANDRY: Imp?

OWENS: Imp!

LANDRY: You think the office has one?

OWENS: Could be. Living in the supply closet and coming out at night.

LANDRY: *(Pointing off, worried)* The supply closet?

OWENS: Behind the notepads and pens and post-its. Peeking from behind weekly planners. Surviving by chewing on erasers and slurping copier toner.

LANDRY: An imp—

OWENS: Then wiping the ink from its lips....

(A pause, then quick blackout)

Scene
"Night Lights"

(SANDERS *and* WEAVER, *looking around nervously*)

WEAVER: The little lights.

SANDERS: I know.

WEAVER: The little lights in the dark rooms. On the copiers and phones, glowing red or green or yellow in the dark.

SANDERS: Like they want something from us.

WEAVER: On the printers.

SANDERS: Like they know something.

WEAVER: Jesus.

SANDERS: They know the office night.

WEAVER: Glowing in blackened offices.

SANDERS: Empty reception areas.

WEAVER: I don't trust them.

SANDERS: I did in the morning—

WEAVER: But not now.

SANDERS: Not now.

(SANDERS *and* WEAVER *slowly eye around the area, warily. Then quick blackout.*)

Scene
"Fate"

(LANDRY *onstage alone, looking around puzzled*)

LANDRY: Owens!

(*No reply from* OWENS)

LANDRY: Owens!

(No reply from OWENS)

LANDRY: *Owens!*

OWENS: *(From offstage)* Landry—

LANDRY: Where are you, Owens?

OWENS: I'm hiding.

LANDRY: From what?

OWENS: Fate.

LANDRY: You can't hide from fate, Owens.

OWENS: I can try.

LANDRY: You can't—that's why it's fate.

OWENS: Don't tell it where I am!

LANDRY: Doesn't matter.

OWENS: Please!

LANDRY: Fate is what's going to happen no matter what.

OWENS: Jesus.

LANDRY: *It is.*

OWENS: That is *screwed* up.

LANDRY: I know—

OWENS: That's like—*no way.*

LANDRY: It's true.

OWENS: Fate.

LANDRY: Fate.

OWENS: Fate! *(Pause) Don't tell it!*

(Quick blackout)

Scene
"Angels"

(SANDERS *and* WEAVER. SANDERS *is clutching his stomach.*)

WEAVER: What's wrong?!

SANDERS: My stomach—

WEAVER: It's the stress.

SANDERS: It hurts, Weaver.

WEAVER: Yeah?

SANDERS: All inside.

WEAVER: That's good, though.

SANDERS: Good?

WEAVER: That we care so much about our job that it makes us sick.

SANDERS: Yeah…yeah, I guess so.

WEAVER: It's how our parents were, how they worked.

SANDERS: In *their* jobs.

WEAVER: They sacrificed.

SANDERS: Gotta make our parents proud.

WEAVER: They worked hard.

SANDERS: Like us.

WEAVER: All week long.

SANDERS: For years.

WEAVER: For decades.

SANDERS: We can't disappoint them.

WEAVER: My parents are watching from heaven.

SANDERS: Make 'em proud as they stare down.

WEAVER: They're angels now.

SANDERS: You know it.

WEAVER: With soft white wings they wash every day.

SANDERS: With heaven soap.

WEAVER: *(Correcting* SANDERS*)* By licking them. Licking them with their gentle angel tongues.

(Brief pause as WEAVER *looks skyward. Then, emotional and still looking skyward,* WEAVER *makes some licking gestures with his tongue upward toward heaven. Then quick blackout.)*

Scene
"Where's Owens?"

*(*WEAVER *has entered* LANDRY *and* OWENS*'s area. Notices* OWENS *is missing.)*

WEAVER: So where's Owens?

LANDRY: Not sure.

WEAVER: He quit from the pressure.

LANDRY: No.

WEAVER: It's why you should've picked me.

LANDRY: I wanted Owens.

WEAVER: Owens is weak. He went home, I bet. To drink alcohol. Watch T V shows—fake people on a screen. Owens is a loser and knows it now. Got honest with himself. A loser who finally knows he's a loser— that's refreshing.

LANDRY: Go back to your office.

WEAVER: Me?

LANDRY: Or else!

WEAVER: Else?

LANDRY: Yeah.

WEAVER: You're trying to scare me with the word "else."

LANDRY: Now!

WEAVER: What is that, a pronoun?

LANDRY: Might be.

WEAVER: "Else."

LANDRY: Else!

WEAVER: "Else"!

LANDRY: Might be a…a mass noun!

WEAVER: Trying to scare me with a word you don't even know what part of speech it is. *(He starts to exit.)* That's sad, Landry. That is a *sad* piece of intimidation.

(Quick blackout)

Scene
"Shoe Again"

(SANDERS is kneeling down and looking at his reflection in his shoe again. Then WEAVER enters.)

WEAVER: Are you talking to your shoe?

SANDERS: *(Startled and defensive)* Uh—no.

WEAVER: You were talking to your shoe.

SANDERS: No, no—who'd do that?

WEAVER: You were!

SANDERS: I was tying it—

WEAVER: *(Pointing at shoe, urgently wanting to know)* What did it say?

SANDERS: Weaver—

WEAVER: *(Grabbing SANDERS and urgently wanting to know)* What did it say?!

(Quick blackout)

Scene
"Dreams"

(LANDRY and OWENS. OWENS has nodded off.)

LANDRY: Owens!

OWENS: *(Startled awake)* Huh?!

LANDRY: No dozing off!

OWENS: I had a dream about the Chairman.

LANDRY: Don't want to hear it.

OWENS: We were walking on a pier—

LANDRY: *Don't want to hear it.*

OWENS: Maybe it's important—

LANDRY: No.

OWENS: On a pier next to a stormy sea—

LANDRY: No dreams, Owens! I've heard the *last*
of everybody's dreams. *(Scoffing)* Freud and the
subconscious. Well, Freud was Austrian, Owens.
Those were *Austrian* brains. Brains made from opera
and chocolates. We got *real* brains, brains that work
on the real level, not some "sub" one full of crap from
fairy tales. Wanna live in a fairy tale? In a gingerbread
house with gumdrop doorknobs? Those doorknobs get
sticky! Be an ugly duckling that grows to be a swan?
(Mocking) Oh, fancy swan! Well, swans drink from the
same ponds they poop in! *(LANDRY thrusts some papers
at OWENS.)* Now go copy these.

*(Lights come up hard on SANDERS and WEAVER also.
WEAVER has also thrust some docs at SANDERS. The next
two lines are played simultaneously.)*

OWENS: Me?   SANDERS: Me?

LANDRY: Just do it!   WEAVER: Just do it!

(Lights off on WEAVER *and* LANDRY, *and light up on* OWENS *and* SANDERS *downstage center as they rush to the copy machine.)*

SANDERS: Outta my way.

OWENS: Outta *my* way!

SANDERS: I'm using the copier.

OWENS: *I* am.

SANDERS: You made the off-center copies.

OWENS: I've got skills.

SANDERS: You're skills are *special needs!*

OWENS: *(Waving docs)* Our ideas for the Chairman!

SANDERS: *(Waving his docs)* Better ones!

OWENS: Landry and I are firing you two!

SANDERS: You can't!

OWENS: When we're promoted!

SANDERS: Never!

OWENS: *(Re his docs)* The new part of our plan!

SANDERS: You're dumb, Owens.

OWENS: Me?!

SANDERS: As dumb as a fart in a jar!

OWENS: *My* copier.

SANDERS: Mine!

OWENS: You're a failure!

SANDERS: *(Re* OWENS*)* A bust!

OWENS: A double-sided—

SANDERS: Tray-jamming—

OWENS: Misfed—

SANDERS: *Error three!*

(Quick blackout)

Scene
"Breakthrough"

(SANDERS and WEAVER. WEAVER looking at some documents excitedly. SANDERS fatigued.)

WEAVER: *(Re documents)* My god, look at these!

SANDERS: I want to sleep—

WEAVER: Not yet, Sanders.

SANDERS: My eyelids are heavy—

WEAVER: Fight it.

SANDERS: It's hard to stand—

WEAVER: More coffee!

SANDERS: My hands are numb—

WEAVER: Stay awake!

SANDERS: Blood too tired to circulate. Pillows, Weaver. Stuffed with the whitest down from the deadest geese.

WEAVER: *(Re a document he's holding)* Have you seen this data set before?

SANDERS: Where?

WEAVER: *(Pointing)* That!

SANDERS: No.

WEAVER: They buried it.

SANDERS: Jesus.

WEAVER: The company had it. Had it but killed and buried it.

SANDERS: Like an upstart princess!

WEAVER: They were idiots! These numbers are just what we need.

SANDERS: You sure?

WEAVER: The missing piece! We run all our figures again with this data and our proposal's the winner!

SANDERS: Now?

WEAVER: *Now.*

SANDERS: *(Re watch, worried)* Time is almost up—

WEAVER: *(Thrusting documents at* SANDERS*)* Fast, Sanders, fast!

(Quick blackout)

Scene
"Half-Asses"

*(*LANDRY *and* OWENS. OWENS *is standing holding the lens section of an overhead projector.)*

OWENS: *(agitated and waving the lens section)* Where's the rest of it?!

LANDRY: What?

OWENS: Where's the rest of the overhead projector?!

LANDRY: Dunno. *(Pointing off)* The A/V department—

OWENS: *(In a building rant)* We need it for our presentation. Goddamn this place! Who let this happen? *Who?!* Bureaucrats, that's who. Slack nine-to-fivers. I'll kill 'em, I will! Why is this office so full of them? The second rate, the C-plussers, the semi-wits! And they all work on *our* support staff. Support? *Support?!* We support *them!* We bring in the cash so they can sit all day refining their incompetence, anuses digging deeper and deeper into their seat cushions. The meek will not inherit the Earth, oh no. The half-

asses will! The world is nothing but half-asses. The
continents half-assed, the countries half-assed. It's half-
assed people in half-assed towns with half-assed pets
and half-assed country clubs with half-assed members
backwashing their hepatitis into gin-and-tonics. They
go to half-assed churches with half-assed heavens,
heavens full of half-assed angels looking down on
all the half-asses doing their half-assed screwing, the
vigorous copulation of the mediocre, over and over,
parts slapping and splatting, thurping and squirting,
making little zygotes—little half-assed zygotes that
pop out, shake off placenta, and rule us all!!!

(Quick blackout)

Scene
"Overnight Markets"

(WEAVER urgently hands SANDERS a sheet of data.)

WEAVER: *(Re the sheets)* The overnight markets.

SANDERS: *(Re data)* Jesus.

WEAVER: *(Re data)* Look at us!

SANDERS: The losses.

WEAVER: Steep, steep ones.

SANDERS: The future forecasts—

WEAVER: Say there is no future.

SANDERS: Our stock price has melted.

WEAVER: Like a popsicle up the Devil's ass!

(They notice a yellow light that has hit them.)

SANDERS & WEAVER: *(Together, surprised and alarmed)*
The sunrise.

(Quick blackout)

Scene
"Sunrise"

(OWENS *and* LANDRY *in yellow light looking out window.*)

OWENS: The morning!

LANDRY: Jesus—

OWENS: Rosy-fingered dawn!

LANDRY: The sun.

OWENS: *(Pointing)* A gaseous star, class G2V.

LANDRY: A yellow dwarf.

OWENS: Call someone here a yellow dwarf—

LANDRY: They sue you!

OWENS: But the sun—

LANDRY: The sun!

OWENS: Hot hydrogen plasma.

LANDRY: *Hydrogen!*

OWENS: And some helium.

LANDRY: Screw helium! Helium is inert, useless—like us if this *(Waving proposal)* doesn't win. We have to be the hydrogen. Explosive energy. What bombs are made of. Bombs that can level whole cities and their pleasure gardens.

OWENS: I'm sure we've got it.

LANDRY: You think?

OWENS: It's all there now. We're going to *whip 'em!*

LANDRY: Like slaves when that was perfectly acceptable!

(Quick blackout)

Scene
"Done"

(LANDRY, OWENS, SANDERS, and WEAVER all onstage. Each holds a thick proposal document in their hand. A sense of great rivalry.)

ALL: *(Holding up their proposals)* Done!

OWENS: *(Holding up LANDRY and OWENS's proposal)* Our proposal!

WEAVER: *(Holding up SANDERS and WEAVER's proposal)* Ours!

SANDERS: The crisis solved!

LANDRY: After the long night's work.

WEAVER: Now we go up there.

OWENS: To the Chairman's.

SANDERS: To that floor.

LANDRY: The elevator doors opening—

OWENS: We step off—

WEAVER: And move forward.

LANDRY: Past receptionists.

SANDERS: Plants.

OWENS: Abstract sculptures.

WEAVER: Along the buffed wood floor.

LANDRY: Our leather shoes—

SANDERS: Striding—

OWENS: Past secretaries lifting their eyes—

LANDRY: Their hands—

OWENS: Standing and pushing phone buttons in alarm!

WEAVER: Down the hall—

SANDERS: Our proposals held high.

OWENS: The vice-chairmen—

WEAVER: Stepping from their offices—

LANDRY: Raising their arms—

SANDERS: Pointing—

WEAVER: Cursing.

LANDRY: The corner suite nearing—

OWENS: Our hearts pounding—

SANDERS: Twelve yards away—

WEAVER: Nine yards—

LANDRY: Six—

SANDERS: Three!

OWENS: The Chairman's office—

ALL: *(Meaning arrived)* There!

WEAVER: We turn the door handle—

LANDRY: It opens—

SANDERS: A draft comes out—

OWENS: Smelling of air-conditioning—

WEAVER: And power!

LANDRY: We hand it to him.

OWENS: He smiles!

SANDERS: *(Holding up proposal document)* The salvation of the company—

LANDRY: *(Waving proposal)* From us!

WEAVER: *(Waving proposal)* Us!

OWENS: Us!

ALL: To the elevators!

(The lights go black as they exit. The sound of rushing feet, but in the darkness voices can be heard.)

SANDERS: I get to push the button.

OWENS: *I* do.

LANDRY: Me!

Scene
"The Chairman's Floor"

(A transitional sound cue of rising urgency and anticipation. Then the sound of a big elevator "ping" and the other sound cue stops and the lights rise hard. LANDRY, OWENS, SANDERS, and WEAVER tumble out of the elevator onto the Chairman's floor. They all look around, suddenly hugely confused.)

SANDERS: *(Distraught)* It's empty.

LANDRY: *(Shocked)* They're gone.

WEAVER: They all left.

OWENS: No one.

SANDERS: The Chairman—

LANDRY: The vice-presidents—

WEAVER: The secretaries.

OWENS: Gone.

LANDRY: *(Calling out)* Hello?!

OWENS: *(Calling out)* Anyone?!

LANDRY: They took their plants—

SANDERS: Their staplers—

WEAVER: The pictures of their dogs.

OWENS: Dead phones.

LANDRY: Silent copiers.

LANDRY, OWENS, SANDERS, & WEAVER: *(Together)*
Nothing.

SANDERS: Office doors left open.

WEAVER: Drag marks on the carpet.

SANDERS: Empty hanging files.

OWENS: Corridors littered with ballpoints.

LANDRY: Brass fasteners.

WEAVER: And little trombones.

SANDERS: They took the tape from the tape dispensers.

OWENS: The art is gone.

LANDRY: *(Re the art)* The landscapes.

WEAVER: The red triangles.

SANDERS: The nudes.

OWENS: There were nudes?

LANDRY: Yep.

WEAVER: We didn't get nudes.

(A pause as they take in their situation.)

SANDERS: They knew.

WEAVER: They knew, so they fled.

SANDERS: We're finished.

OWENS: All our work.

LANDRY: Gone.

WEAVER: Our careers.

SANDERS: Over.

OWENS: Our stock shares.

LANDRY: Worthless.

WEAVER: Everything from last night.

SANDERS: Useless.

(Pause)

WEAVER: How could this—?

LANDRY: How?

WEAVER: Maybe if we'd been faster.

LANDRY: *(To* OWENS*)* If *we'd* been faster.

SANDERS: Finished while they were still here—

OWENS: Before they fled like cowards!

WEAVER: Like lemmings!

SANDERS: Like the worst things you could possibly compare them to!

WEAVER: *(Waving proposal)* Our proposal would've saved us.

OWENS: *(Scoffing)* Ha!

LANDRY: *(Waving his proposal)* Ours would have—

SANDERS: *(Waving his proposal)* Ours!

LANDRY: Never!

WEAVER: *(Waving his proposal)* This one!

OWENS: *(Waving his proposal)* This one!

SANDERS: This!

LANDRY: This!

WEAVER: *This!!*

(As WEAVER *says "This!!" he swings and hits* OWENS *with the proposal. The proposal bursts into parts and powder and dust. Then they all start hitting each other with the copies of the proposals, all of which burst in the same way. It's a big dusty melee. Then, after several moments of fighting, they all separate, their anger spent, their suits and the floor covered in the dusty remnants of their proposals. They grimly and glumly take in their situation. After a moment,* WEAVER

speaks, looking at the floor and the dusty remains of the proposals.)

WEAVER: They're nothing.

OWENS: Dust.

LANDRY: Like our careers.

(Pause)

SANDERS: Dust.

WEAVER: Like our lives now.

(A pause, then OWENS turns forward and points.)

OWENS: The window.

(They all turn and look forward. Then they all slowly get a brave, determined look on their faces, and crouch, poised to run forward, then all run forward with a shout. A blackout and the loud sound of shattering glass, then lights up on the four falling, with sound of wind.)

Scene
"The End"

(LANDRY, OWENS, SANDERS, and WEAVER all falling from the building. The growing sound of wind speed as they plummet, all four looking around and down, taking in their fall. After a moment, LANDRY speaks.)

LANDRY: What's the forecast on gravity?

(The sound of the rushing wind grows more, the sound cue becoming more elaborate, suggesting both falling and a kind of transcendance, the looks on the four's faces growing even more alarmed. After another moment or two SANDERS starts to sing to lift their spirits.)

SANDERS: I've been working on the railroad, all the live long day—

(OWENS joins in. Lights begin to fade.)

OWENS & SANDERS: I've been working on the railroad—

(WEAVER *joins in.*)

OWENS, SANDERS, & WEAVER: Just to pass the time away.

(LANDRY *joins in.*)

ALL: *(With lights fading more away)*
Can't you hear the whistle blowin'
Rise up so early in the morn.

(*The lights to black.*)

ALL: Can't you hear the captain shouting,
Dinah blow your—

(*The sound cue cuts off sharply. A beat. Then lights up hard on curtain call as curtain call music plays loudly. Suggested curtain call song: the Clash's "Career Opportunities."*)

END OF PLAY

www.ingramcontent.com/pod-product-compliance
Lightning Source LLC
Chambersburg PA
CBHW052206090426
42741CB00010B/2435